3 Step Budgeting

Basic Budgeting Made Easy

By

Maro Ross

Contents

Dedication

To all those who want to improve their station in life

<u>Acknowledgements</u>

The author would like to acknowledge everyone throughout my life who has contributed to my success. We truly are each other's teacher and student.

Introduction

Let's face it many of us were not taught how to budget. Our introduction to the word budget often comes with no instructions on how to do it. Ignorance, desires, and a society that promotes spending without constraints has created an environment where budgeting is no longer taught or cherished. So you may have a few questions.

What can you expect to gain from this EBook?

Money power. Money isn't everything but it takes money to do just about anything. Budgeting helps your direct and hold on to more of your cash.

Why should I listen to you?

Experience. I have been a part of the financial industry for nearly a decade, as a salesman and collector; I begin to notice patterns of why people failed. One such pattern was no budget. This information, about how to budget, has made a positive difference in my finances and I believe it will do the same for you.

Do I have to learn a lot of financial lingo?

No. In many cases I skip over financial terms. It is more important to learn the concept and enjoy the benefits. Should you decide to advance your financial skills this will provide a bases of understanding.

Money has a way of leaving if not told were to go ahead of time. The purpose of a budget is to keep more of your money and to also channel it to the areas of your life that gives meaning and joy.

Step one is about inflow. Inflow is all the money you receive in a given time period. You will learn how to gather your inflow information. You will also learn what data to use from your inflow research to make a budget.

Step two is about outflow. Outflow is all the money that departs from you in a given time period. In this step you will learn how to keep track of where the money goes.

Step three is about creating your budget. A budget is a plan to direct money before you get it. In this step you will use your inflow and outflow information to make decisions.

Budgeting is your partner in helping you live the life your dreams. The better you are at directing and keeping money, the more of your hopes and desires will be fulfilled.

Step One

Inflow Information

Know how much you get

Years ago I had an opportunity to talk to a man who owed a large sum of money. While talking to him on the phone he became more agitated.

Me: "How much of it can you pay right now?"

Man: "I don't know" (little agitated)

Me: "Why don't you know?"

Man: "Cause I don't know how much my paycheck will be" (more upset)

Me: "Can't you make a logical guess?"(beginning to get agitated myself)

Man: "What part of I don't know you don't understand" (hangs up)

This Chapter you will learn different ways of gathering inflow information, an essential step before you can make a budget.

Paystubs

Paychecks often come with a receipt. This receipt is what is called a paystub. What's important about this paystub is the information that it shows. Generally the stub is broken up into major sections. Some typical sections are:

1) General Information
2) Tax Data
3) Paycheck Summary
4) Earnings
5) Taxes
6) Before Tax Deductions
7) After Tax Deductions
8) Employer Pay Benefits
9) Net Pay

It is a good idea to make sure that all information in you paystubs is correct. Let's look at the last category.

Net Pay

Net pay is money you receive after deductions are taken. You should focus on the net because this is the money you actually have to work with.

Note: Gross pay is money you get before deductions are taken, your true pay.

Creating Deduction Formula

Unless you are paid a straight amount, e.g. a salary, your pay will likely be different each time. Since budgeting is about directing money <u>before</u> you receive it; you'll need a way to estimate the net pay. Enter the need to create your own deduction formula. Here is the equation:

Average Net ÷ Average Gross × 100 - 100= Deduction Percentage

Let's take a closer look at this equation

Getting Gross Averages

To get your net and gross averages do these steps:

1. Gather your most recent paystubs (at least three, but the more the better)
2. Add up the previous net and gross dollar amounts off your paystubs
3. Then divide by number of paystubs used.

In this example we use six recent paystubs to get gross dollar amounts:

Amounts Taken From Pay Stubs	Gross Amount
Paystub #1	$800
Paystub #2	$750
Paystub #3	$850
Paystub #4	$900
Paystub #5	$650
Paystub #6	$825
Total Gross	$4,775

Take the total gross amount and divided by the number of paychecks. In the example we used 6 checks.

6 ÷ $4,775= $795.83 Gross Average

Now to get the net averages.

Get Net Averages

Net Amount Taken From Pay Stubs	Net Amounts
Paystub #1	$780
Paystub #2	$600
Paystub #3	$680
Paystub #4	$720
Paystub #5	$520
Paystub #6	$660
Total Net	$3,960

6÷$3960=$660 Net average

Now using the average of both gross and net, let's create our deduction formula:

$660 average net ÷ $795.83 average gross=1.21

1.21 × 100= 121

121 – 100= 21% Average Deduction Percentage

In this example 21 is the average deduction percentage. This means going forward you can get a close estimate of what you will receive as net payment.

Say, for example you know you will work 35 hours next week. You make $10/hr. which means you will gross $350 (35 hours × $10= $350). Using the previous example average deduction percentage of 21, you simple take the gross amount and minus it from the deduction percentage to get your net estimate ($350 – 21% = $276.50 net estimate).

You would than use the net estimate in making your budget.

Note: Keep in mind your average deduction percentage can change as the amount of your deductions from your paycheck changes, i.e. put in higher tax bracket, changes in insurance premiums, retirement contributions, etc., so update your average deduction percentage accordingly.

Commission

Commission type pay can be a little tricky. For one, pay amounts are rarely consistent. Second there is usually no set time period for payments received-you only get paid for what you sell not time used to work. So how do you know what to plan for if you are not sure when you get paid and what amount that pay would be?

Averages

A way to tackle commission pay is to come up with an average monthly amount. Though you may not get a pay stub it is likely for tax purpose you get some kind of receipt detailing the pay rendered. You want to gather these receipts. Go back a year or at least past three months. Add up the total net amount than divided by the number of months and you will have a monthly average.

Total net amount ÷ number of months= commission monthly average

It is commission monthly average that will be the bases for inflow information.

Tax Records

If you are in a bind not having paystubs or other forms of receipts use tax records.

Note: The tax record technique not work well if your current year is not identical to previous year.

To use your tax record just use the previous year gross and use your personal deduction formula which gives you the estimated net amount. Then divide it by the estimated number times you get paid in a year.

To figure out the estimated number of times you get paid in a year just use your pay schedule within a year.

For example: You are paid every two weeks. Using 52 weeks as our bases you can expect to receive 26 pay checks. 52 weeks ÷ 2 (for every two weeks) =26 estimated pay checks receive for a year.

With yearly net pay and estimated pay schedule you now have the information to find out what your average payment will be to make a budget.

For example: $20,000 yearly net ÷26 payments in a year=$769.23 net pay per pay period

The important point about using tax records is to make sure your payment schedule and yearly amount is as accurate as possible.

Other Inflow

We touched on paychecks, commission, and tax records in finding inflow information that can later be used for budgeting. There are other ways people receive money including dividends, retirements funds, and government assistants. In most these cases the principle is the same, know how much you get and how often.

Summary

Inflow is all the money you receive in a given time period. For personal budgeting purposes you should use net pay. The three major ways to find inflow information is through pay stubs, commission receipts, and tax returns.

Step Two

Outflow

You spend more than you think

One of my passions is going to my local discount bookstore. There hardly is a time I walk out of there without buying something. A couple hard- to- find books, used DVD's and an occasional miscellaneous item and I am out the door happy with myself for purchases. Like any good thing, do it too much and it can become a problem. Soon I began to notice that I was spending way more money than I thought. This scenario can happen easily to anyone. In this step we will look at outflow or how much money you spend in a given time period.

Where the money goes

Money is like water, it's able to find its way out of seemingly impossible ways. Trying to hold water in your hands is difficult and money can be no different. Like water, the key to managing your money is harnessing the flow. To do this means to pay attention to where the money goes by tracking outflow. There are many different ways to track and since I am more interested in you understanding the concept first, let's look at the basic components you will need.

Debt

When it comes to outflow there are two main ways money can flow, liabilities is one. I promised earlier that you would not need to be a financial wizard so I will just say that a liabilities is debt. Debt is money that goes to something you are obligated to pay more than once. By far debt is one of the biggest outflow destinations for money, for this reason it is important to keep track of what you owe.

Expenses

Expenses is the second main outflow destination. An expense is money spent one time for one transaction. For example buying milk at the grocery store is a one time, one payment transaction.

For the sake of keeping things simple, you should combine both debt and expenses and just call it outflow.

Recording were the money goes

When I first started out, there weren't a lot of software tools that were easy to understand when it came to tracking my outflow. Today things have definitely changed. I recommend that you invest in software program that allows you to update information with your bank through the internet. Of course if you are not comfortable or don't have the means you can use good old fashion calculator, pencil and paper.

Collect your receipts

Every transaction should have a receipt, even if you have to create one. These receipts should be kept together. The system I use is the envelope. The envelope system works like this. Take a new envelope and write the month and year on the front. Then when you have receipts for that month put it in the envelope.

Logging

In addition to keeping the receipts you must log your transactions. Logging is writing down the transaction information from the receipts. Logging should be done daily. There are three basic informational items you need in order to properly log: date, business, and amount.

Date

Use the date of the transaction. This should be the same as on the receipt.

Business

The business refers to who you exchange money with. It doesn't have to be a business; it could be anyone that you had a financial transaction with.

Amount

How much money was exchanged.

When it comes to logging I use my electronic checkbook on my computer and just keep the receipts in an envelope for up to six months. The six months is an arbitrary number and can be shorter or longer as desired.

Note: You can log also in paper form with the most famous way through a checkbook register. The important point is to update regularly.

Step Three

Budget

The 3 Financial positions

There are only three positions anyone can be in financially. These three positions can and often do change. The three positions are these.

Rich

Rich means that they have more coming in than going out. Out of all the positions this is the best for those who want financial success.

Broke

Broke is when a person has the same amount of money going out as they have coming in. In a sense a person in this position is covering everything they need to cover, which is good, but should there be an unexpected expense, cut in income, etc. they can easily in a poor position.

Poor

This position occurs when outflow exceed inflow. When this happens there is greater temptation to make up the short fall with debt, which for many becomes a trap.

Decide which position you want to be in and then create your budget.

Creating a Budget

Budgeting is telling your money where to go before you get it. With that in mind it is time to get started creating a budget.

Start by using a three ring binder, pencil, and calculator. Next gather all your bill statements that are due in the coming month. If you do not have a bill you can often get a copy from the company website, if that is not possible you will need to do a monthly average using the last few bills or use your best guess to create an estimate. The third step is to calculate how much money you will have in the coming month (see step two for ideas on how to do this). Last is to find a quiet place to do your budget without distractions.

On the binder write budget. Then open the binder and fill it with college rule paper, this will be your budget binder and should be kept in a secure place. Once you have your binder ready it is time to write your budget.

Use pencil or erasable ink when creating your budget so that you can correct your mistakes easily. On the top line write the month and year of the budget.

	August 2013	

Next write your inflow information in the far right side of the page. Remember inflow is all the money you will receive that month. In this example the person will receive two payments of a $1,000 equaling $2,000 for the month.

	August 2013	Inflow
		$1,000
		+ $1,000
		= $2,000

Now you will write down the outflow- date, dollar amount, and who you given the money to.

			August 2013		Inflow
	Rent	$500	8/1		$1,000
	Savings	$100	8/1		+ $1,000
	Grocery	$200	8/1		= $2,000
	Grocery	$200	8/15		
	Utilities	$200	8/20		
	Cell	$100	8/21		
	Dinning	$150	8/25		
	Total	$1,450			

In this example, outflow is less than the income. This gives a surplus, rich position, but what happens when outflow exceed inflow. The solution is to either increase your inflow, or start making cuts. This is the reason for using pencil so you can make adjustments.

Conclusion

Budgeting is a practice that you want to master. Let's go over what we learned.

Step one gathering inflow information. You primarily gather this information through pay stubs. If paystubs are hard to come by you can use your tax return to get an estimate.

Step two tracking outflow. The major way to gather outflow information is through bill statements and receipts.

Lastly, step three, creating a budget. We learned to us inflow and outflow information to create a plan.

Budgeting is something that can be mastered and I hope this has been a help to you. I ask that you let me know if this information was helpful and if there is anything that would make it better. I hope the best for you. Good Luck!

www.ingramcontent.com/pod-product-compliance
Lightning Source LLC
Chambersburg PA
CBHW071603170526
45166CB00004B/1775